Curled Whirled & Twisted

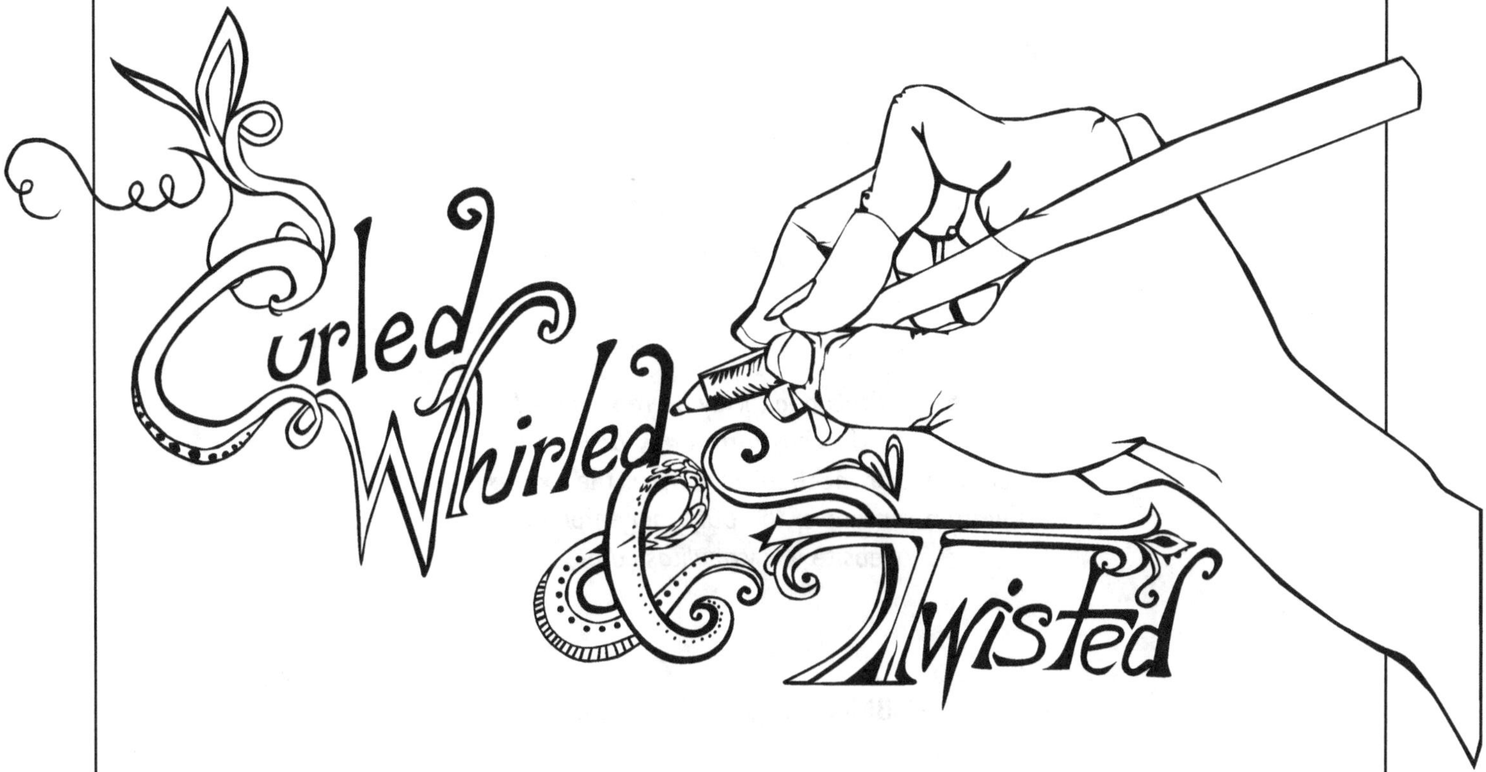

Coloring Pages featuring the art of Jennifer Long de Herrera

Curled, Whirled & Twisted
Coloring Pages featuring the
Art of Jennifer Long de Herrera

ISBN-13: 978-0692553756

ISBN-10: 0692553754

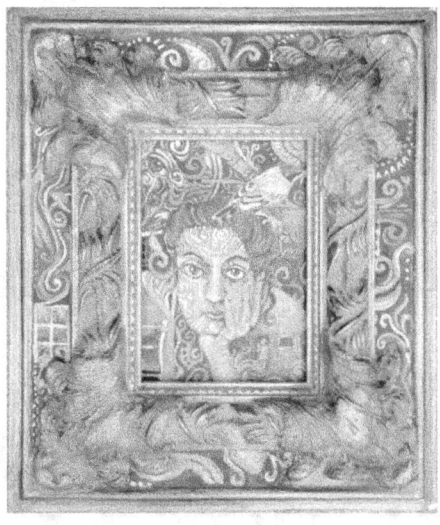

About the artist and the images:
Jennifer Herrera has been making art for as long as she can remember. She was born and raised in the mountains of North Carolina and studied at North Carolina School of the Arts and Appalachian State University before running away to tropical Mexico where she got married and started a family. She currently lives with her husband and two children in the northeast corner of Georgia. To create this book she scanned paintings, drawings and doodles and redrew them digitally. More of her paintings, drawings, and paper mache (including many of the pieces used to create this book) can be seen in full color on her website, www.azulitas.com.

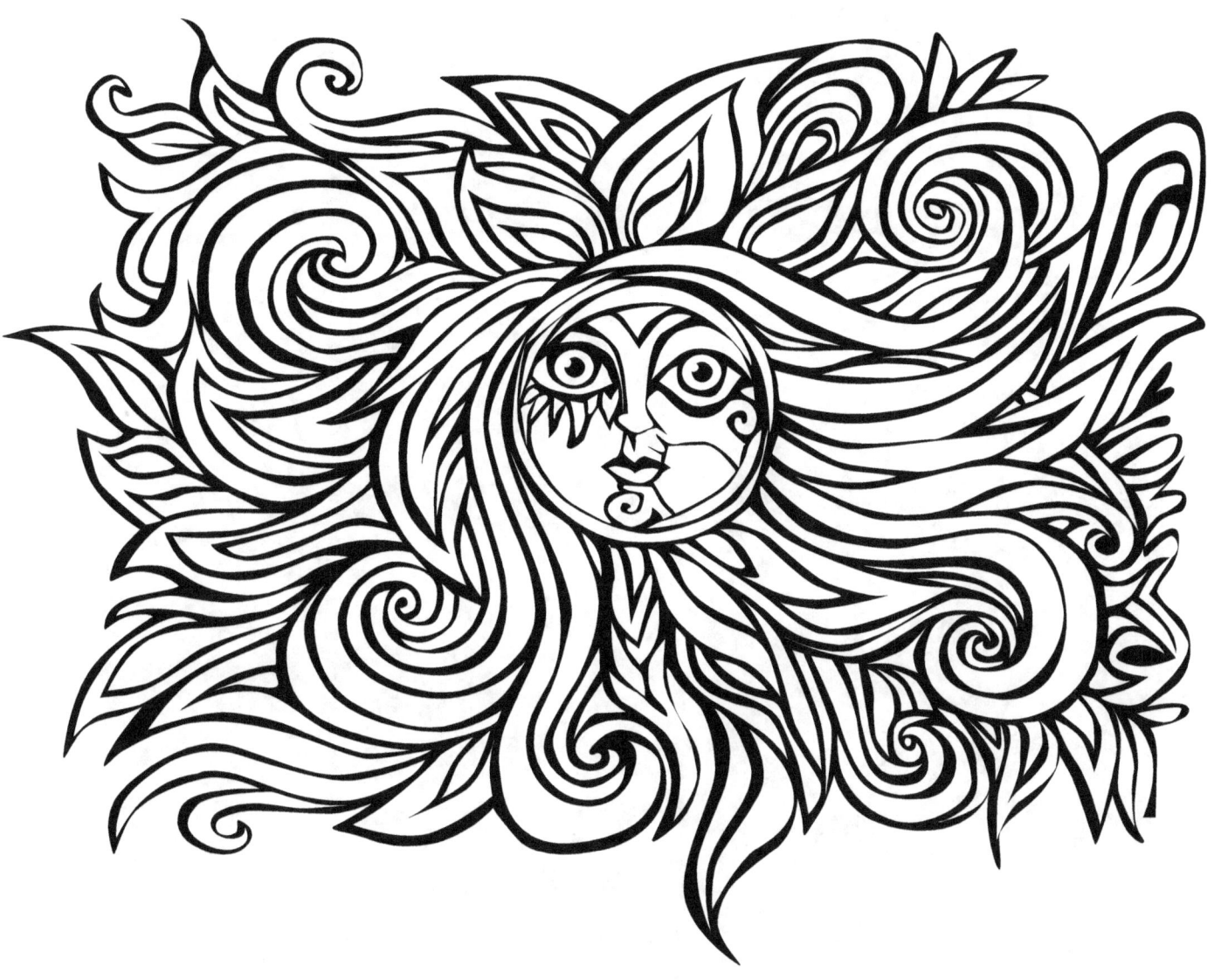

Acoloring book should require no instructions. You know what to do. However, just in case you need it... you have my permission to color outside the lines, to draw your own lines, and to even see what might happen if you find some old-fashioned white-out and remove some lines. Scribble wildly with crayons and highlighters or painstakingly shade with colored pencils or do something else entirely. Creating these images was a pleasure and I hope you find your own joyful and relaxing way to cover them with color.

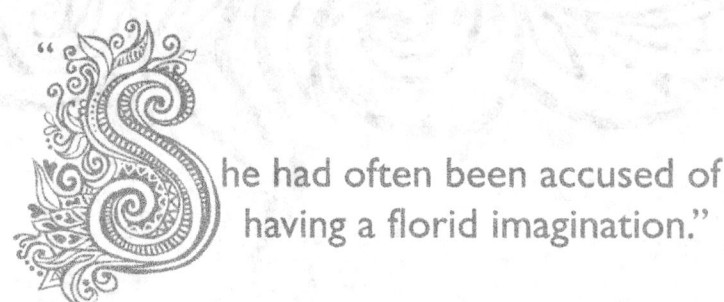

"She had often been accused of having a florid imagination."

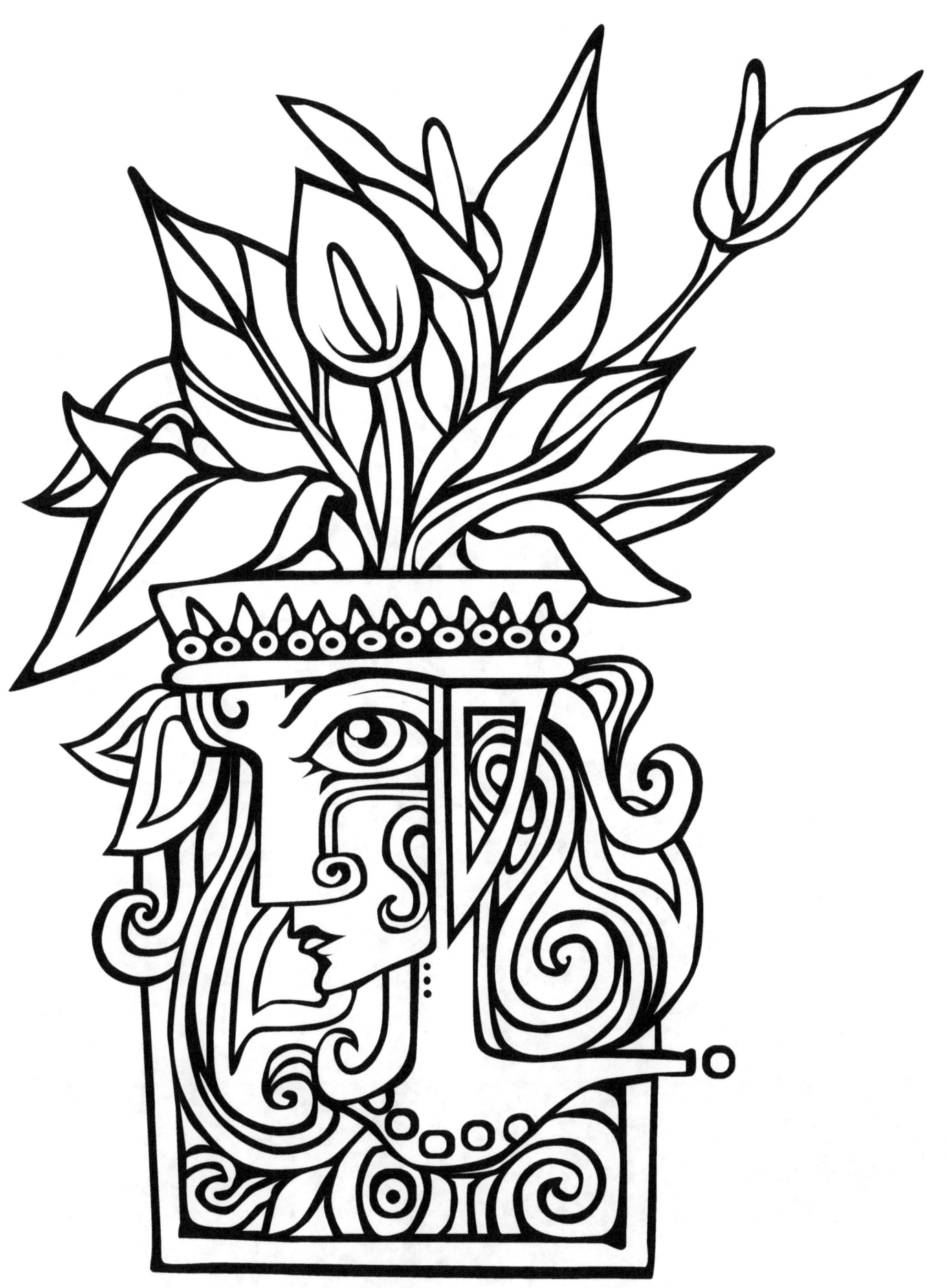

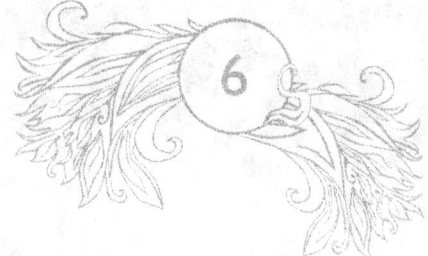

6

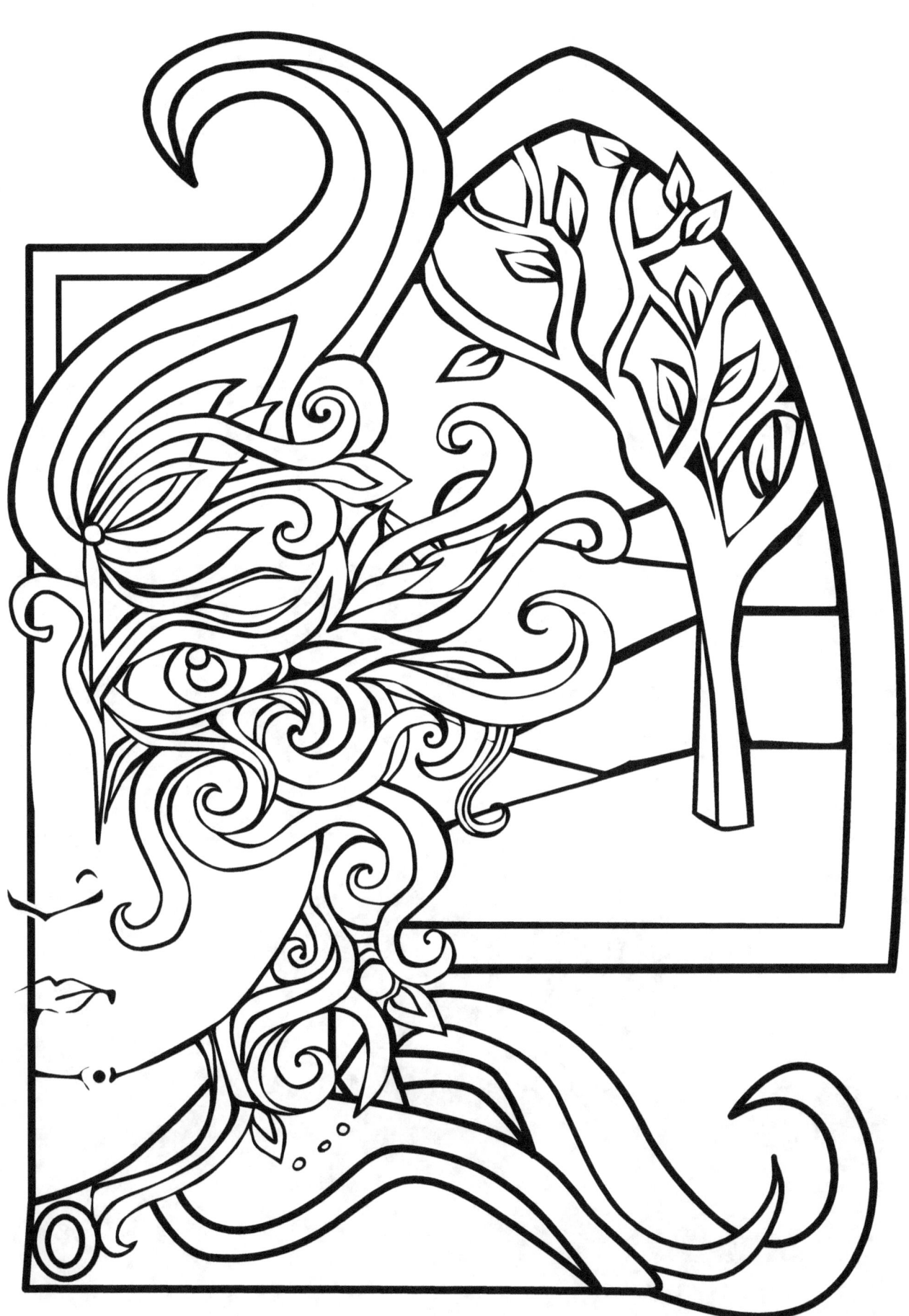

"Blossoming was a rather more peculiar experience than imagined, fleeting yet with perennial possibilities."

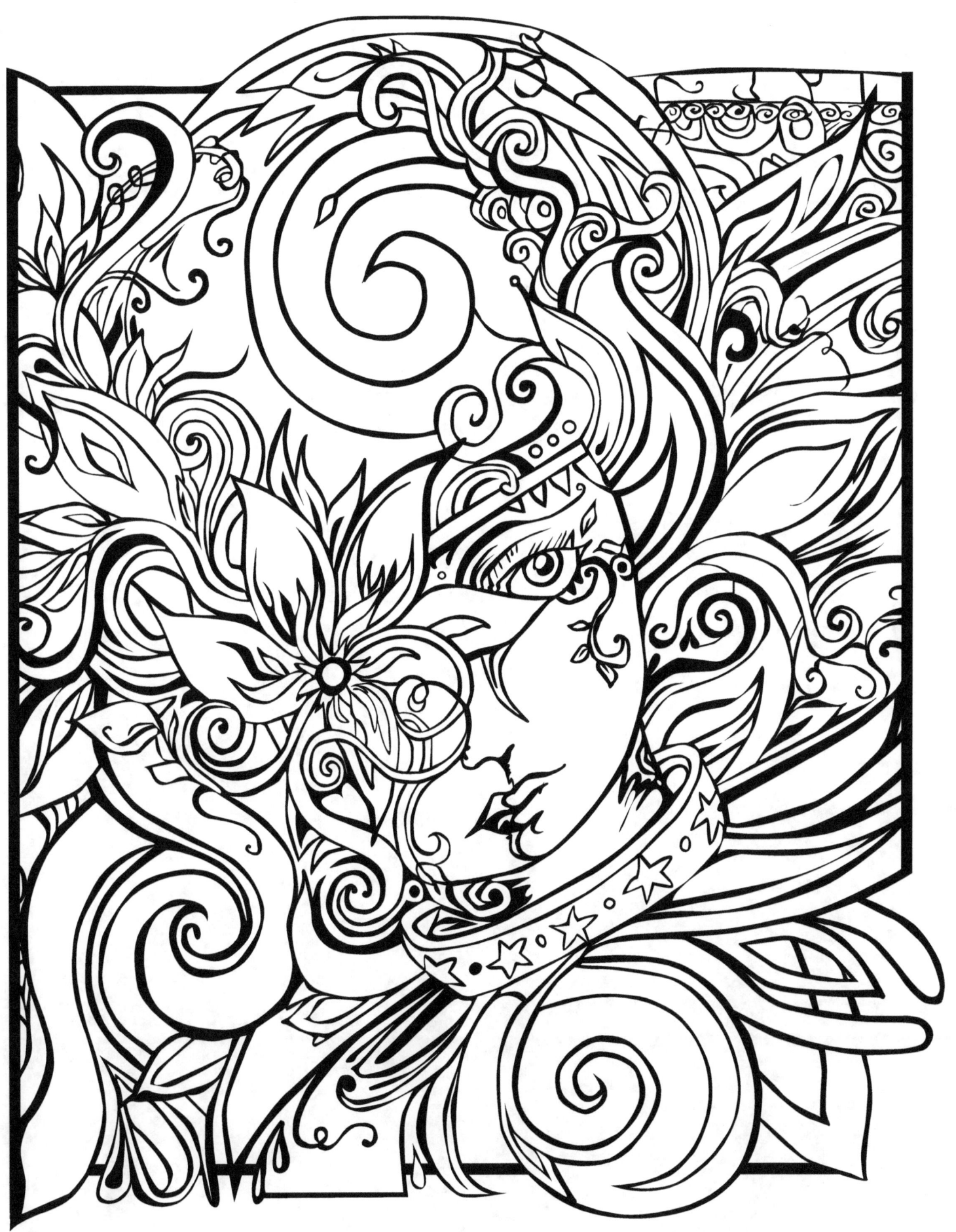

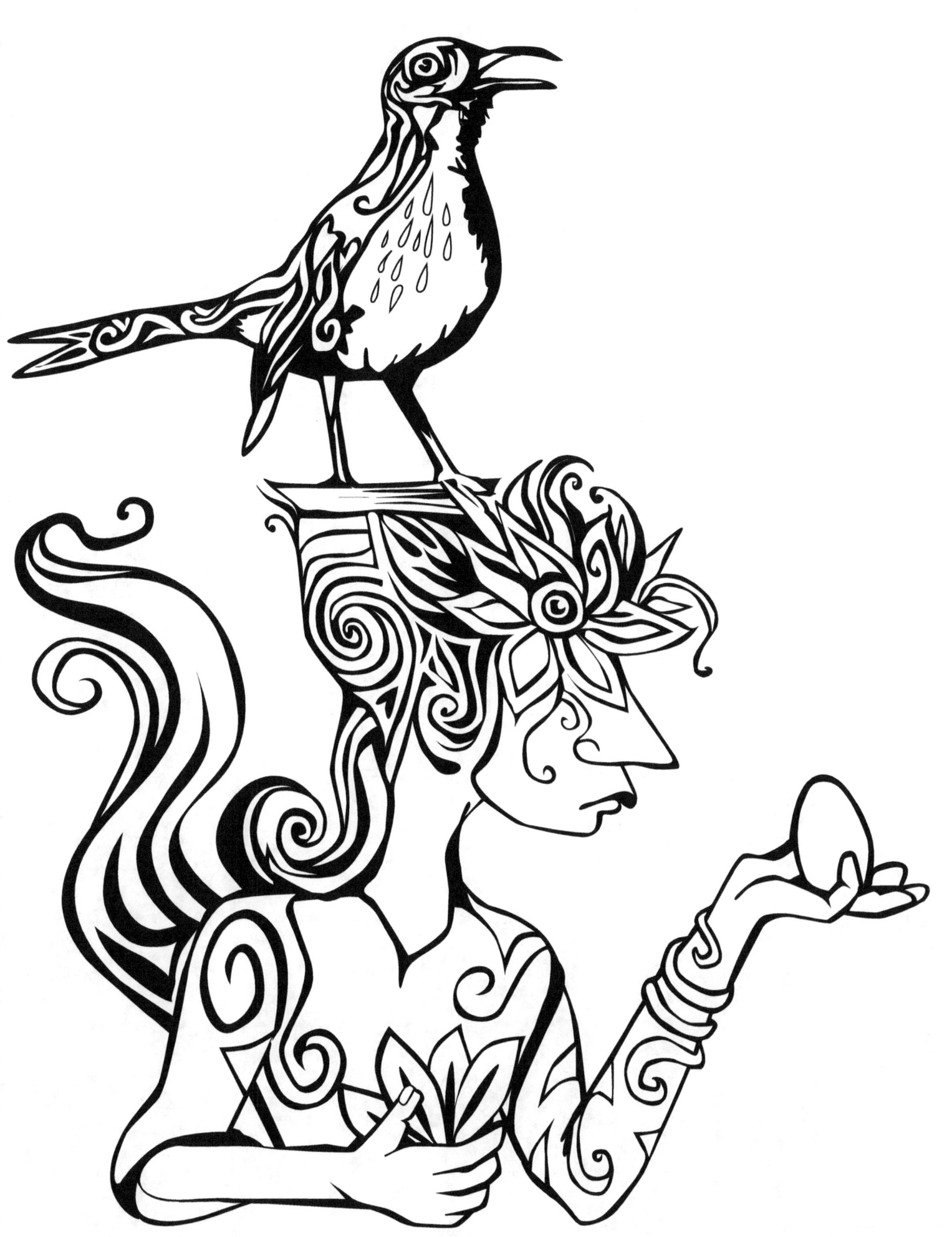

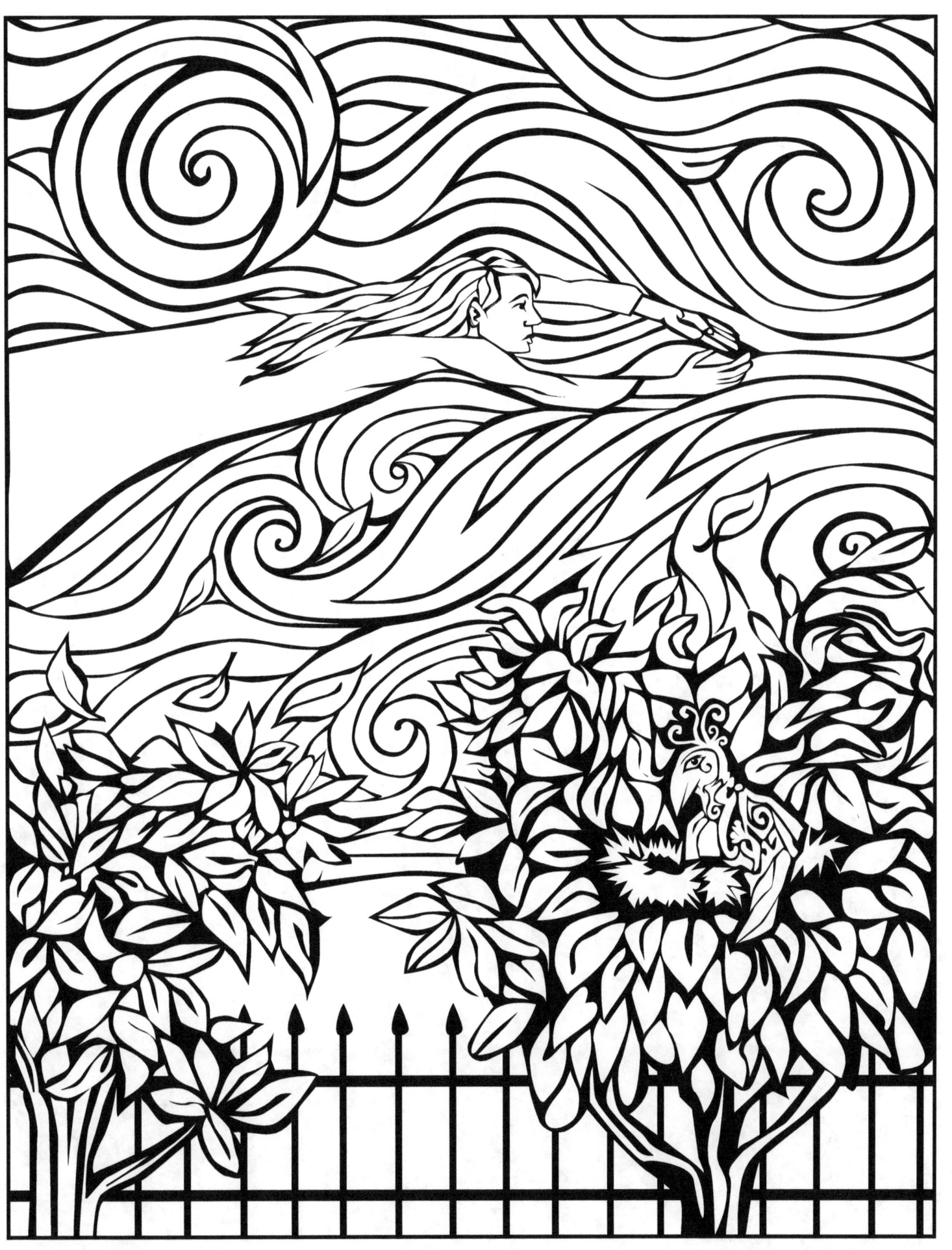

14

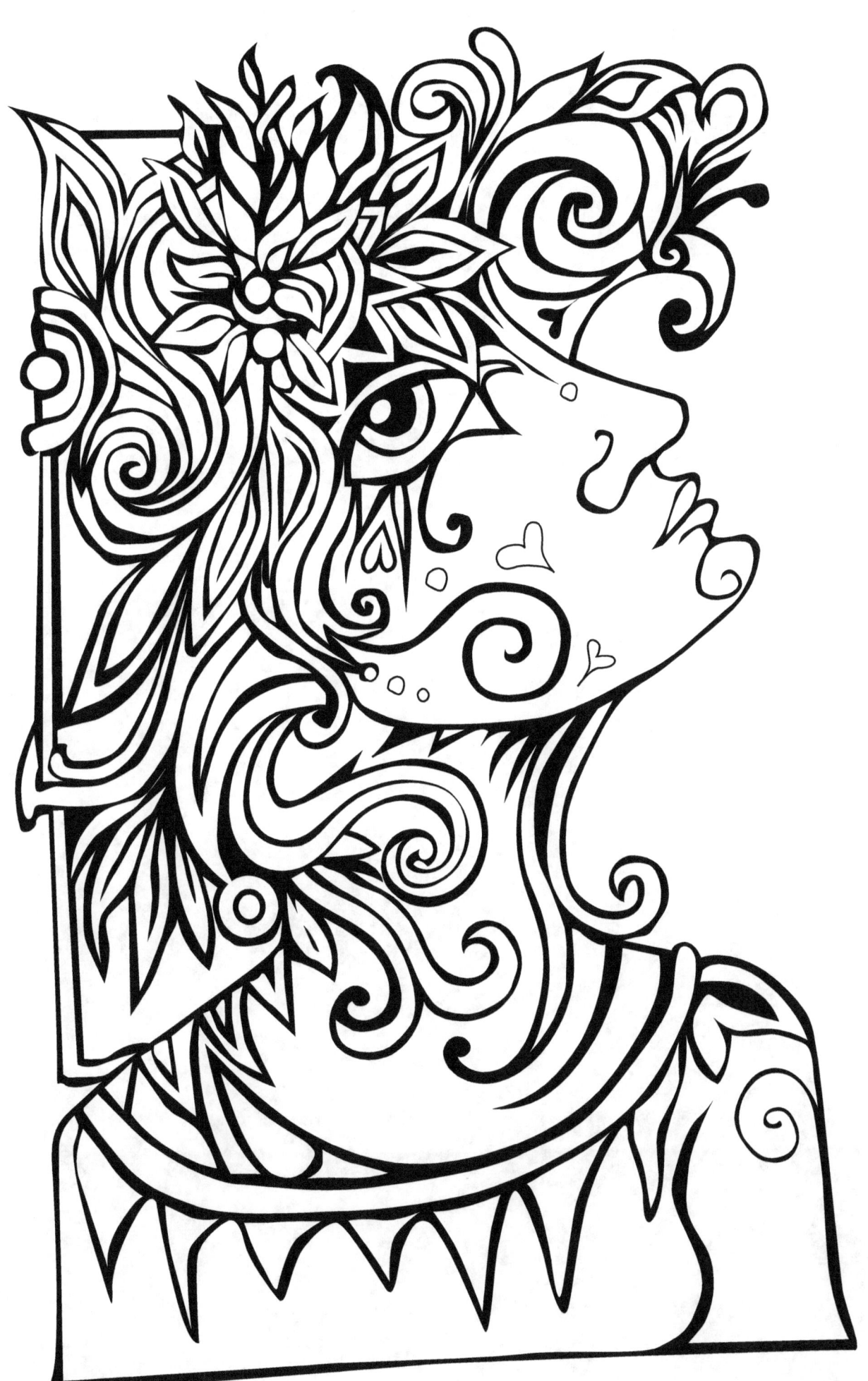

16

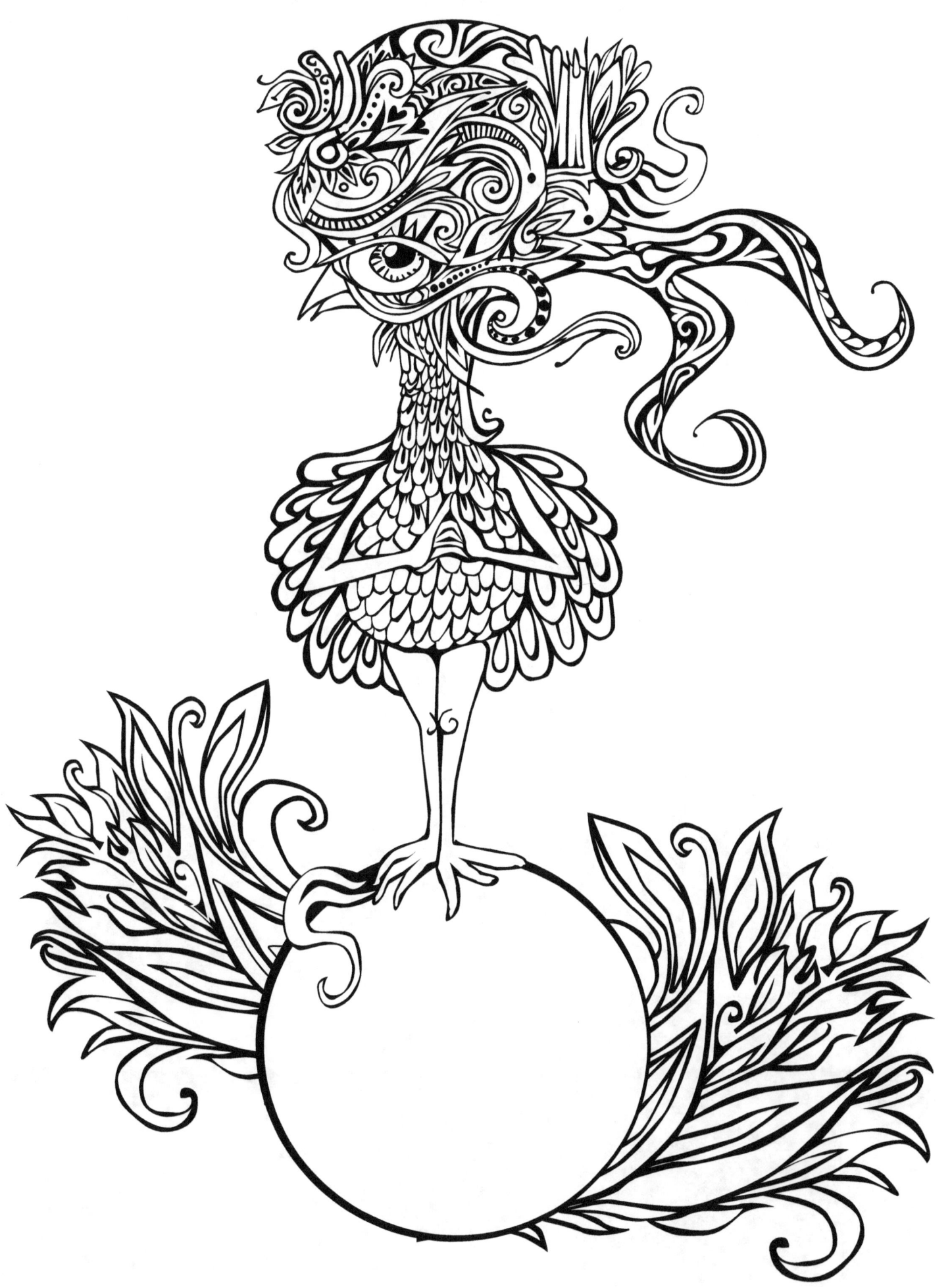

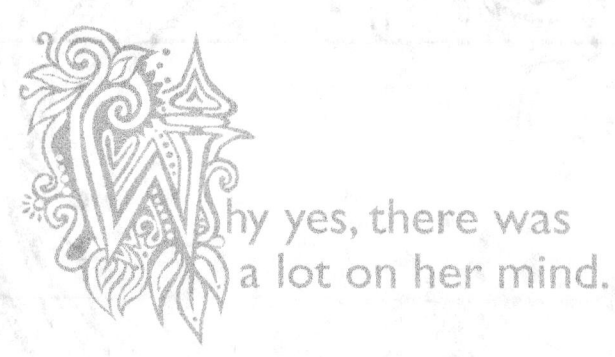

hy yes, there was
a lot on her mind.

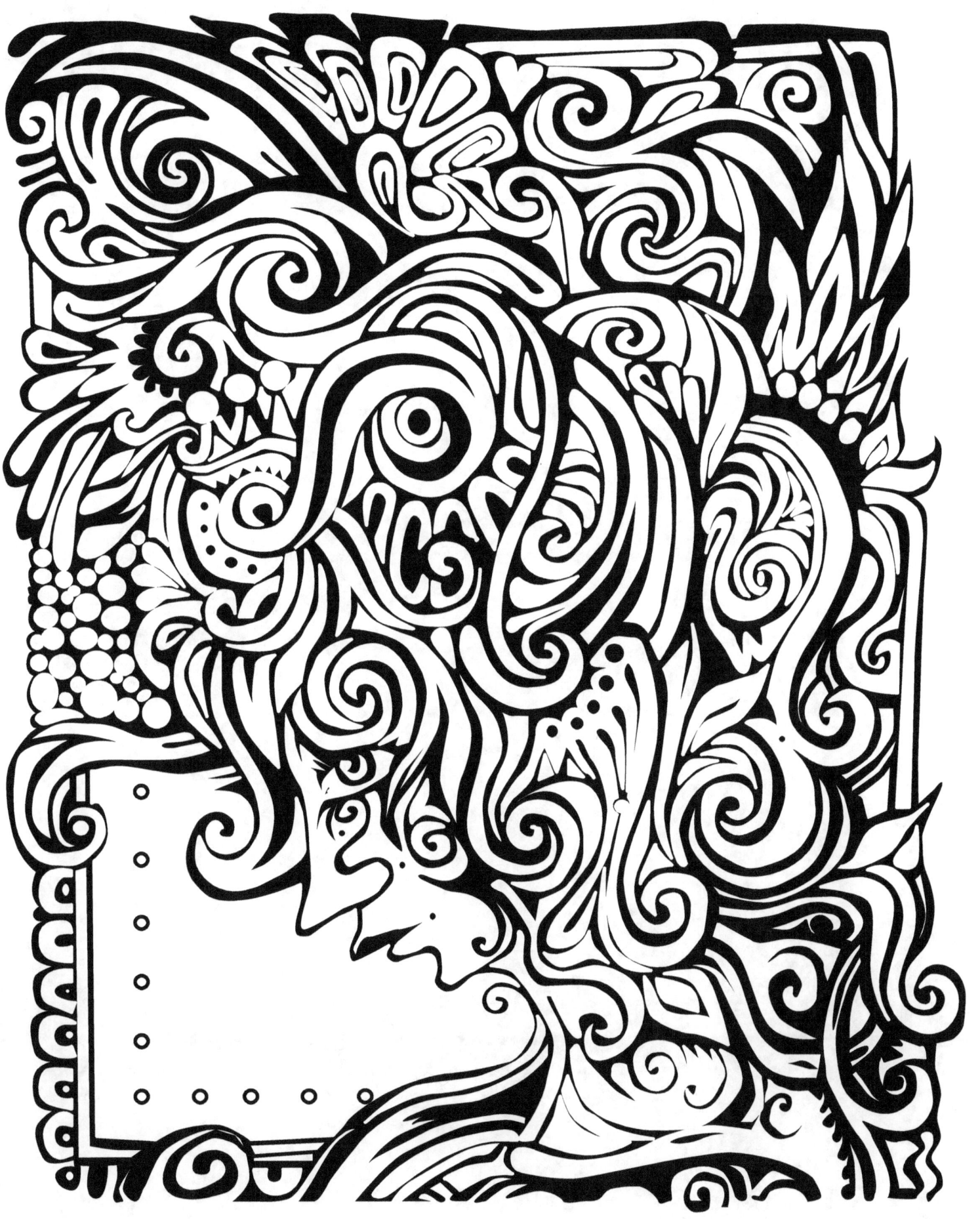

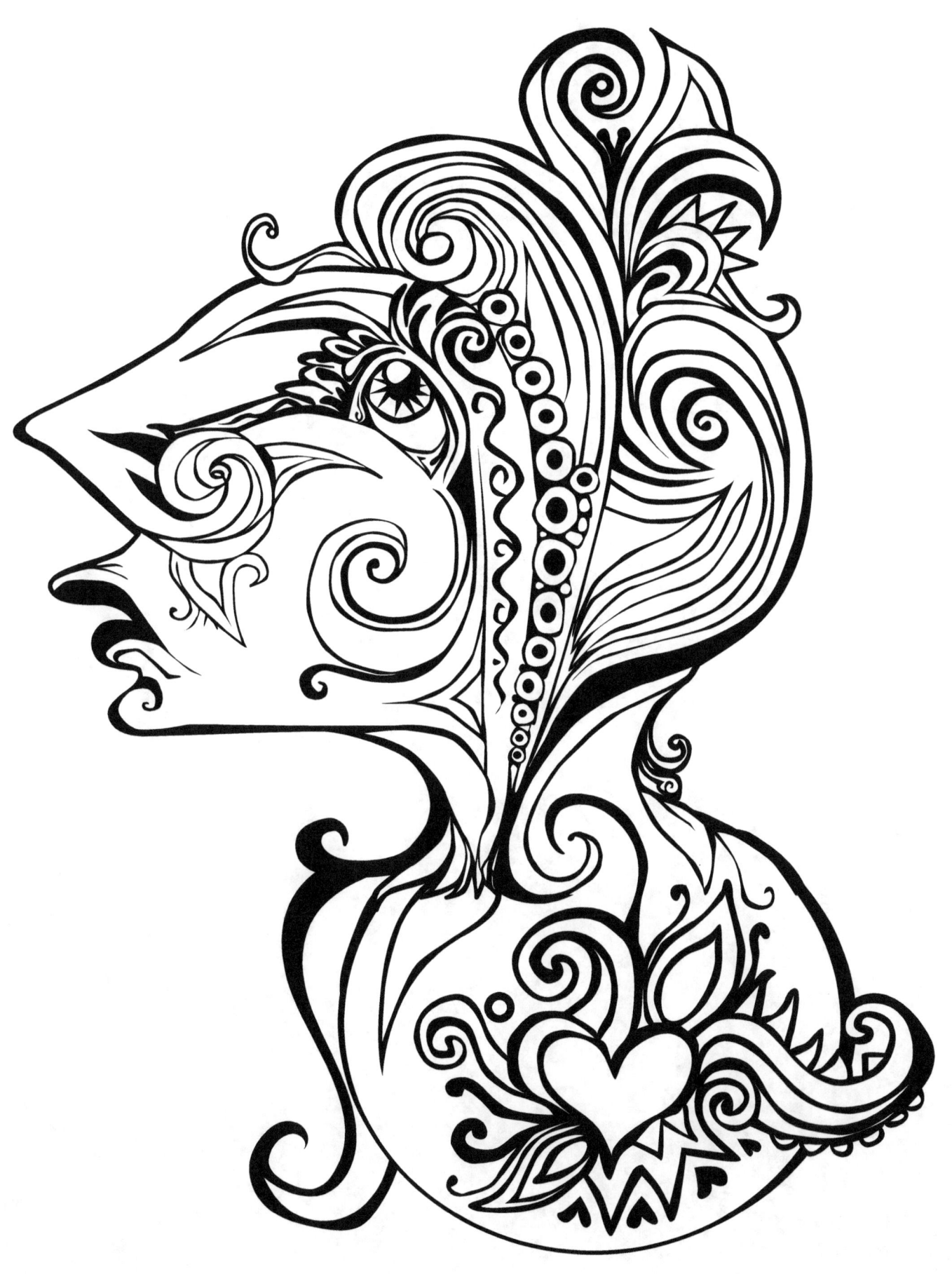

22

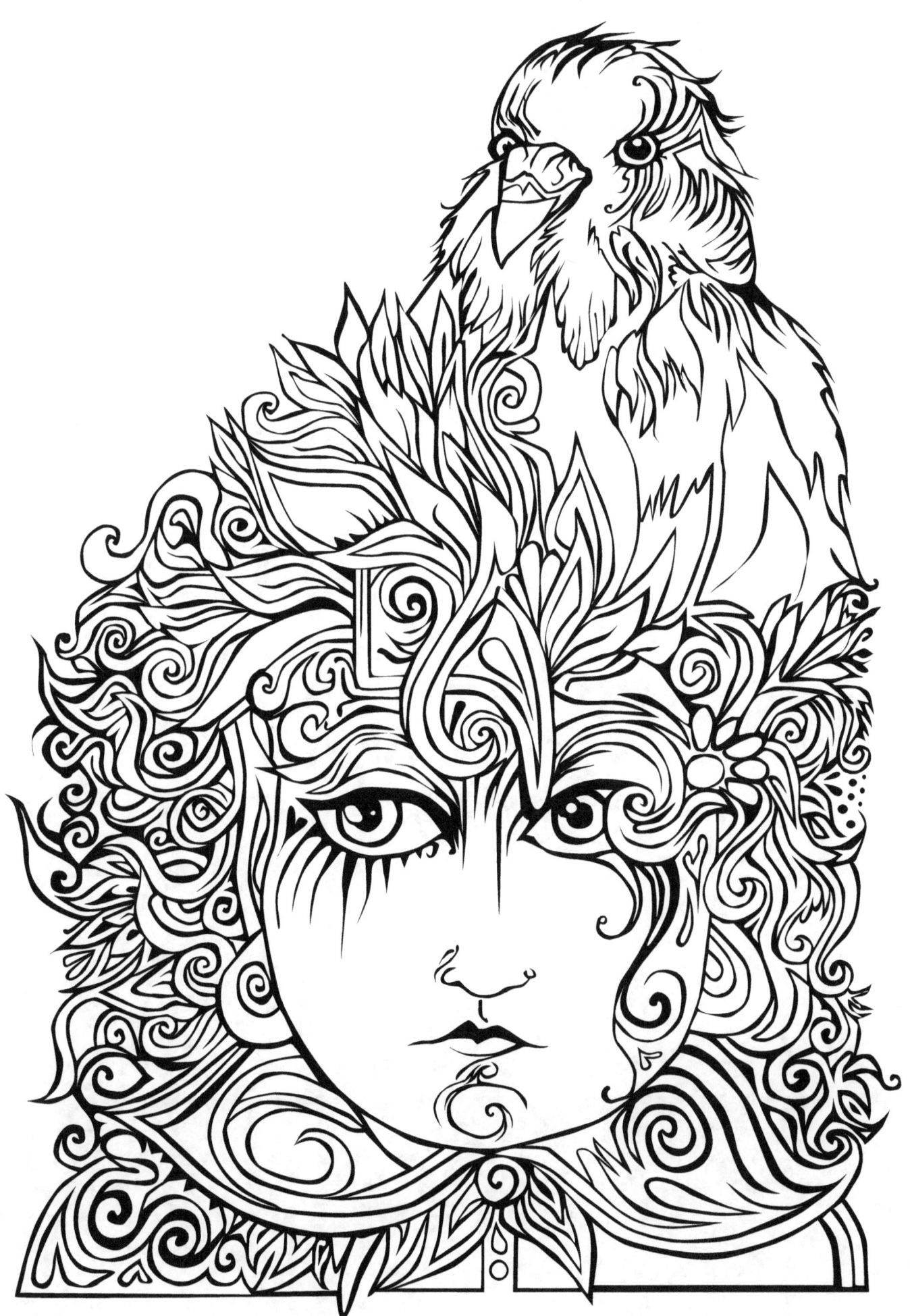

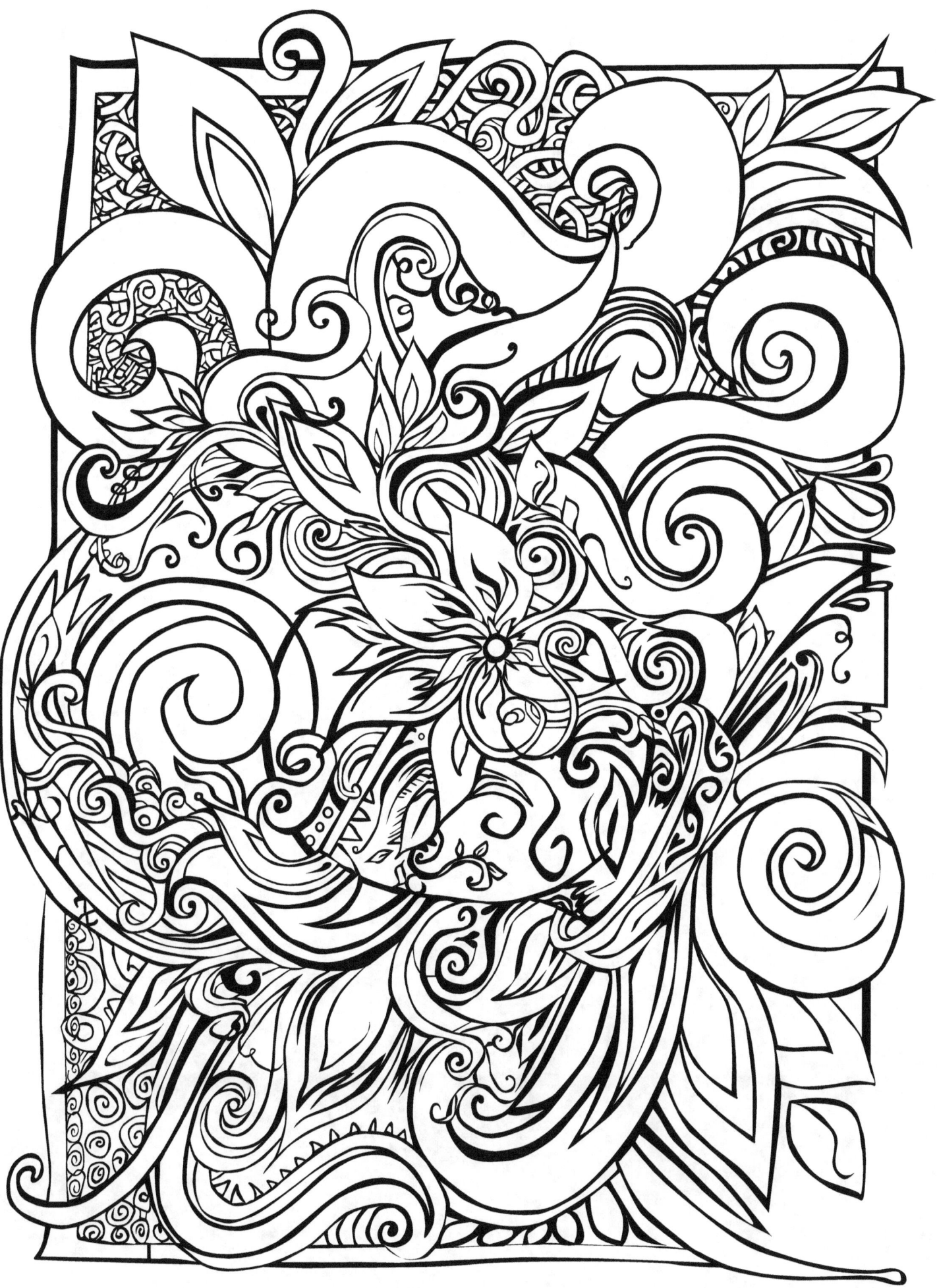

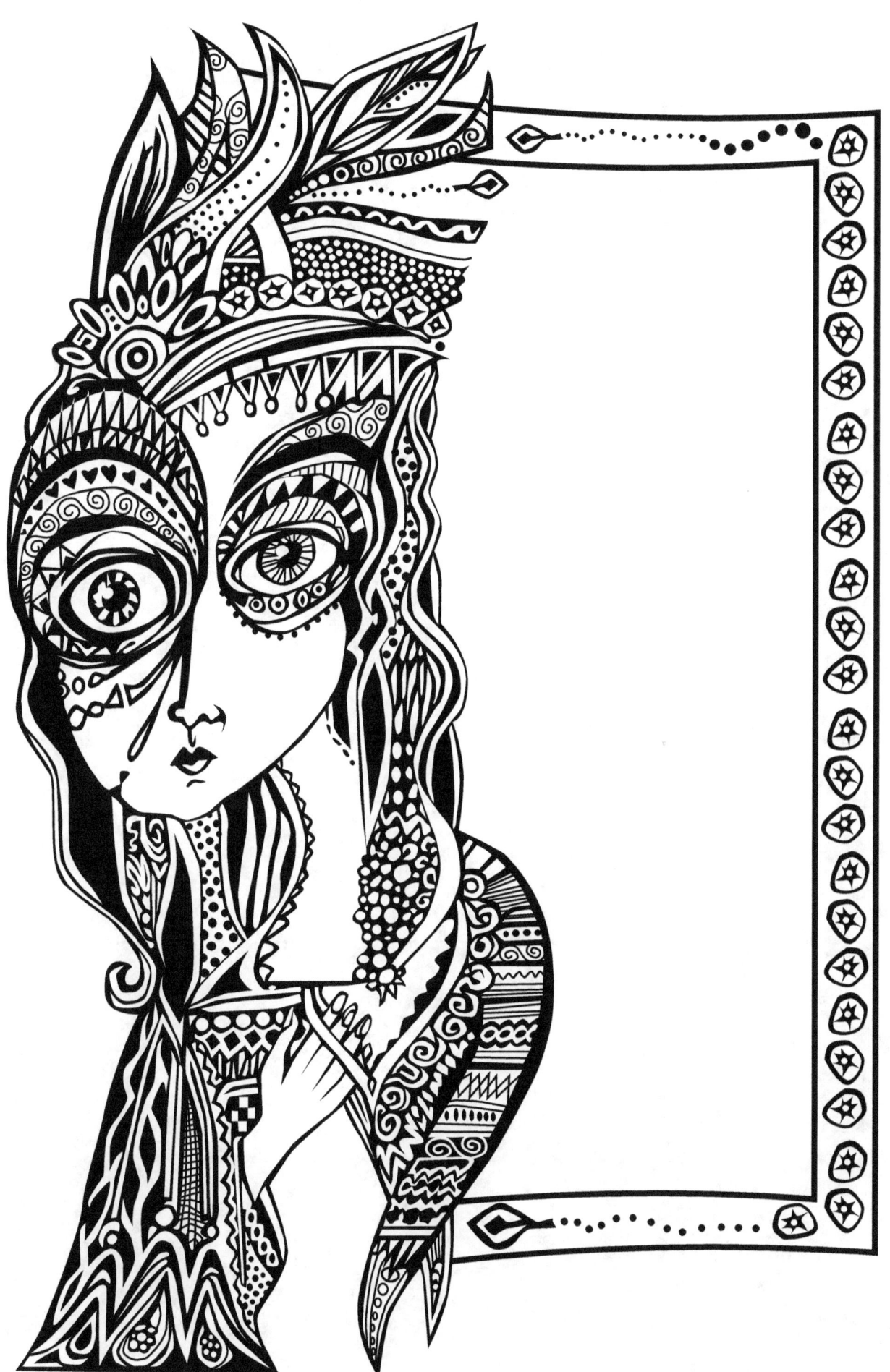

"...and then she no longer described
it as encroaching, but present."

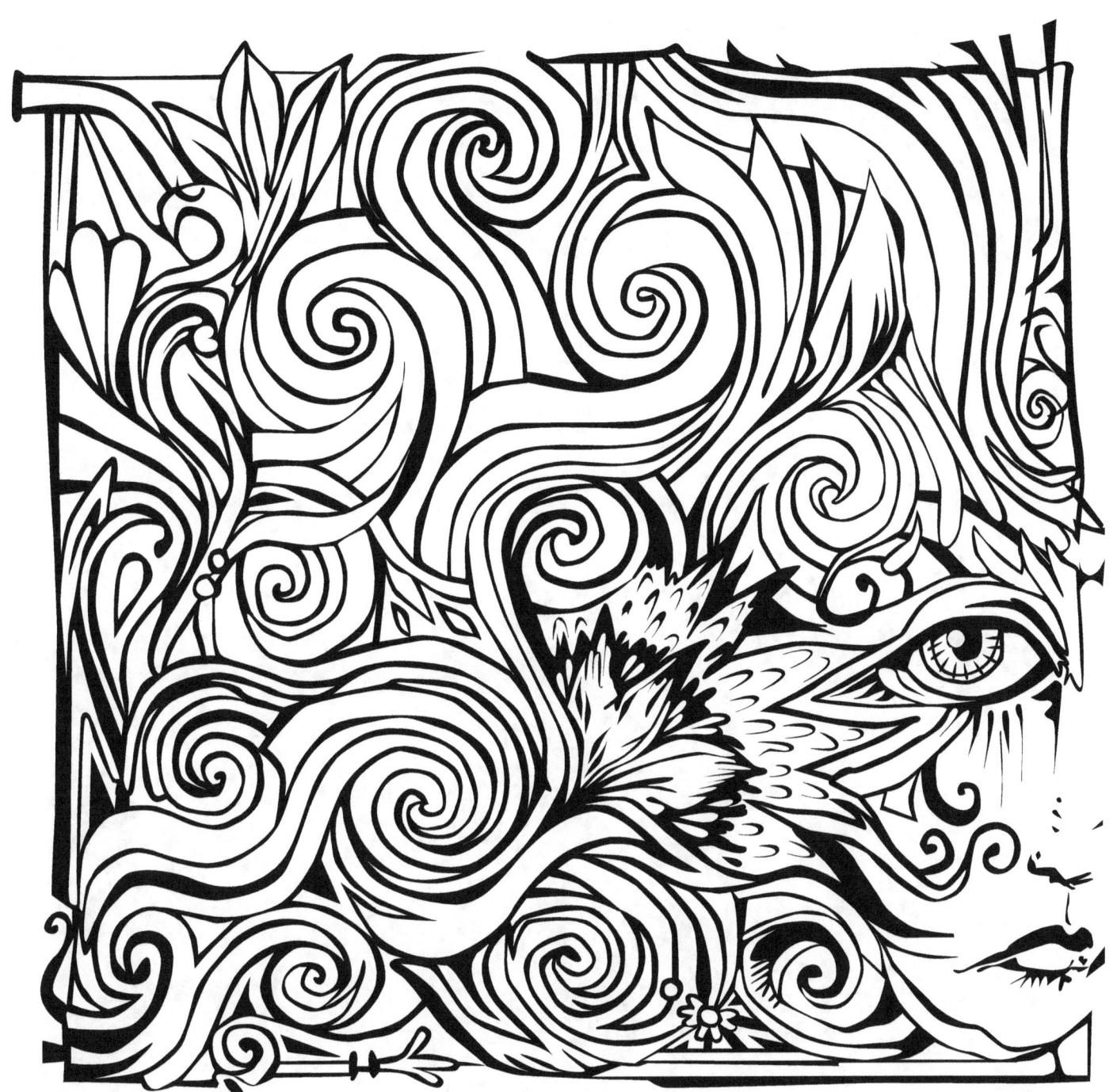

30

Is her hand raised in greeting or in warning?
What might be on the other side of the gate?

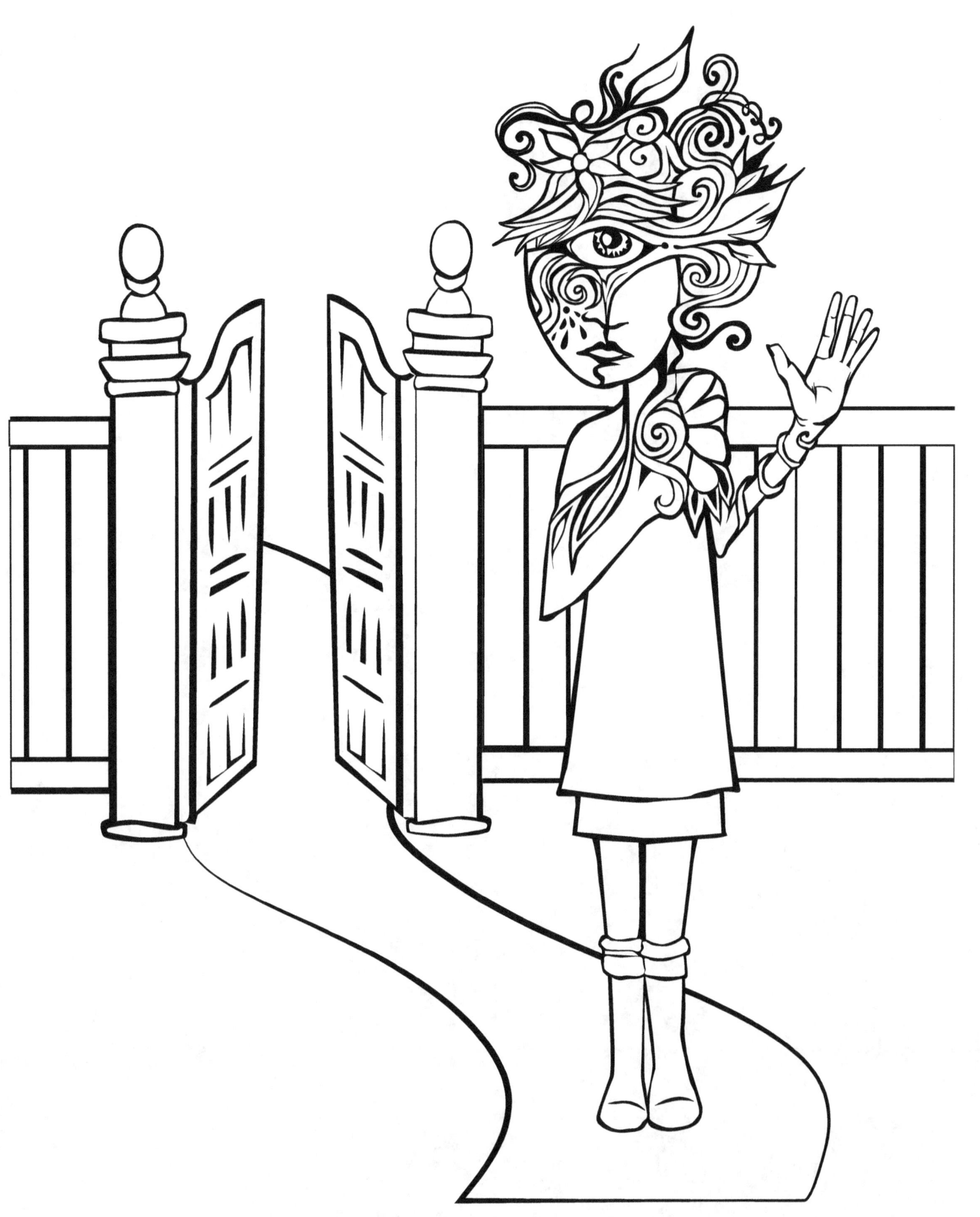

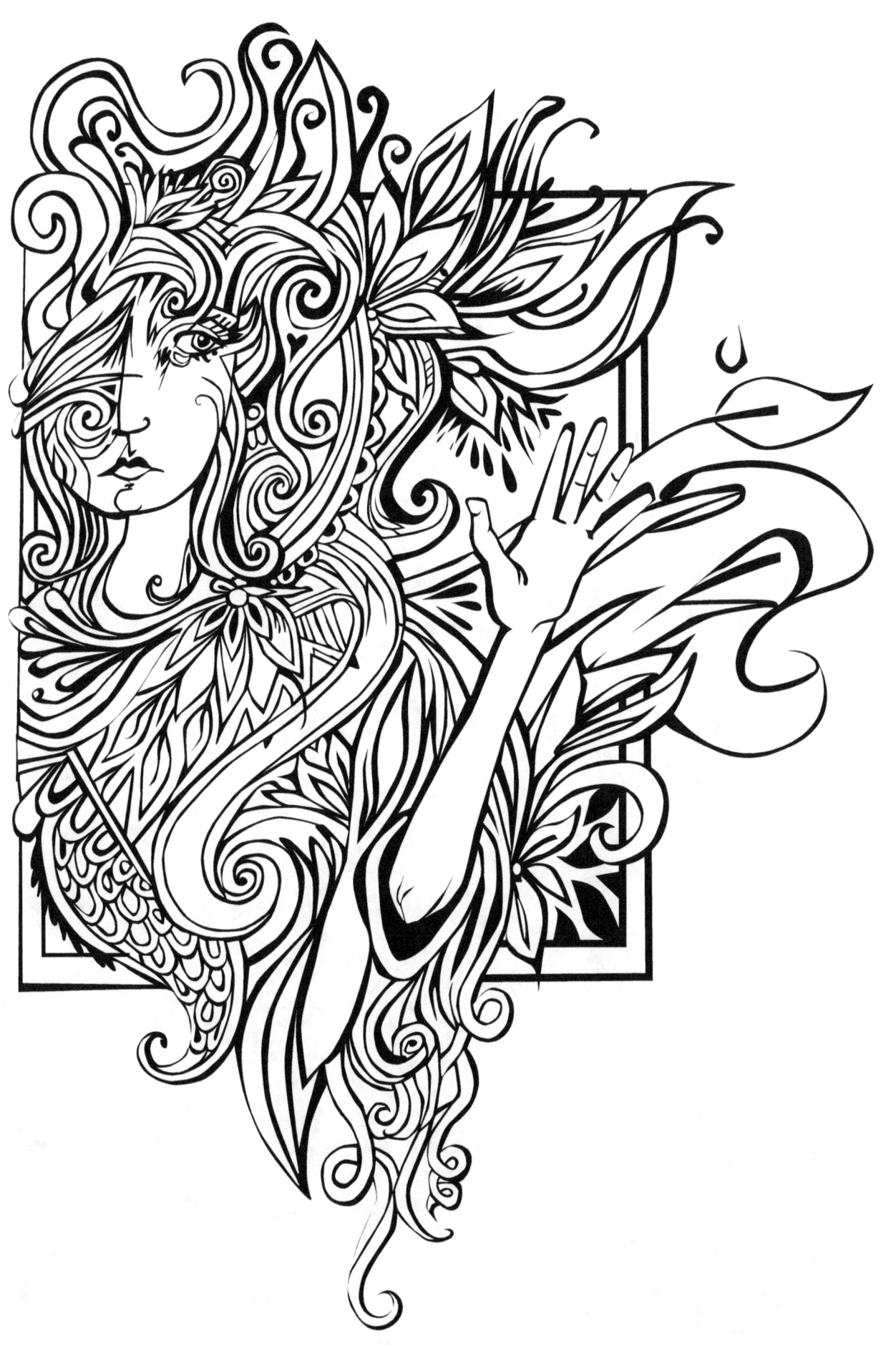

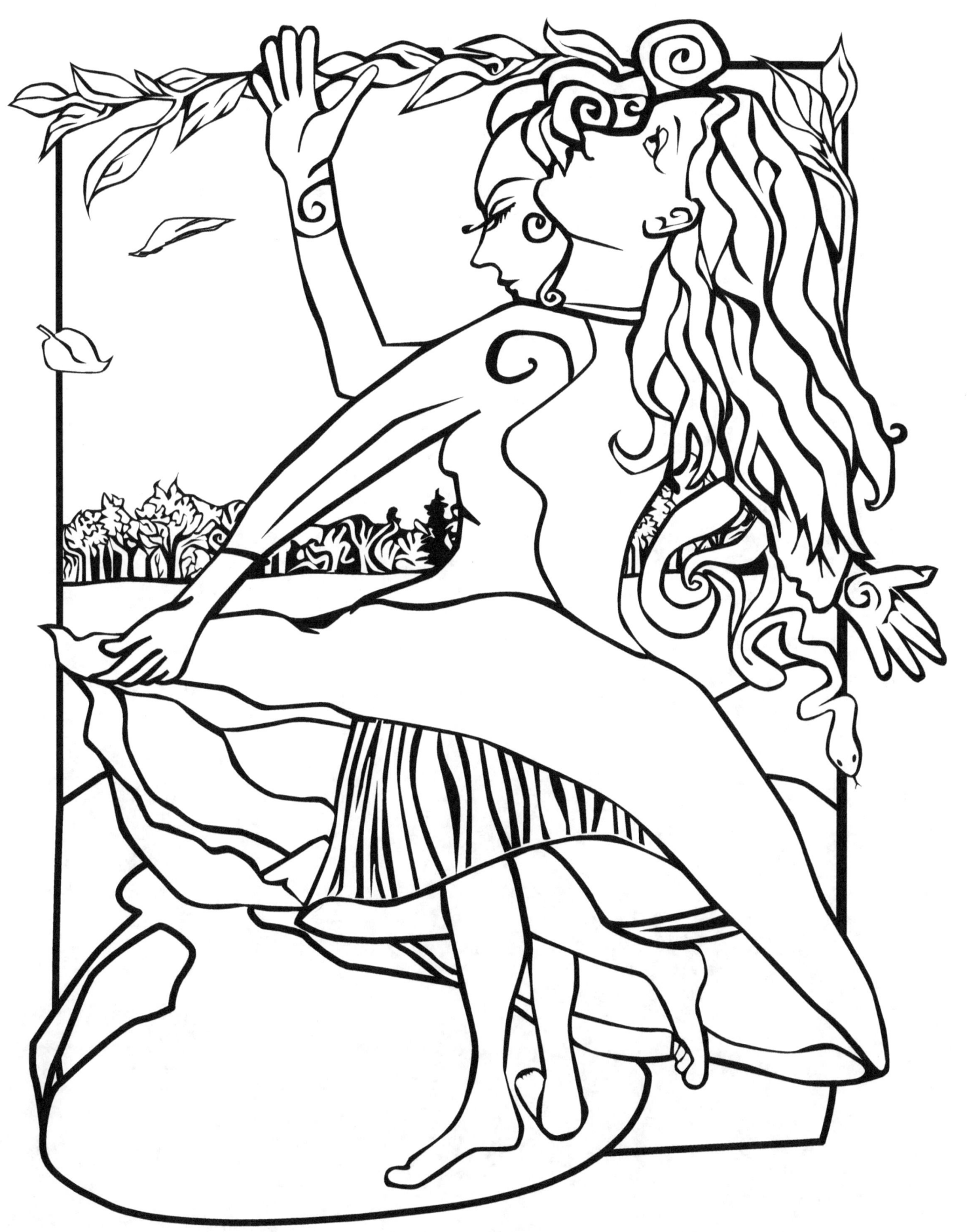

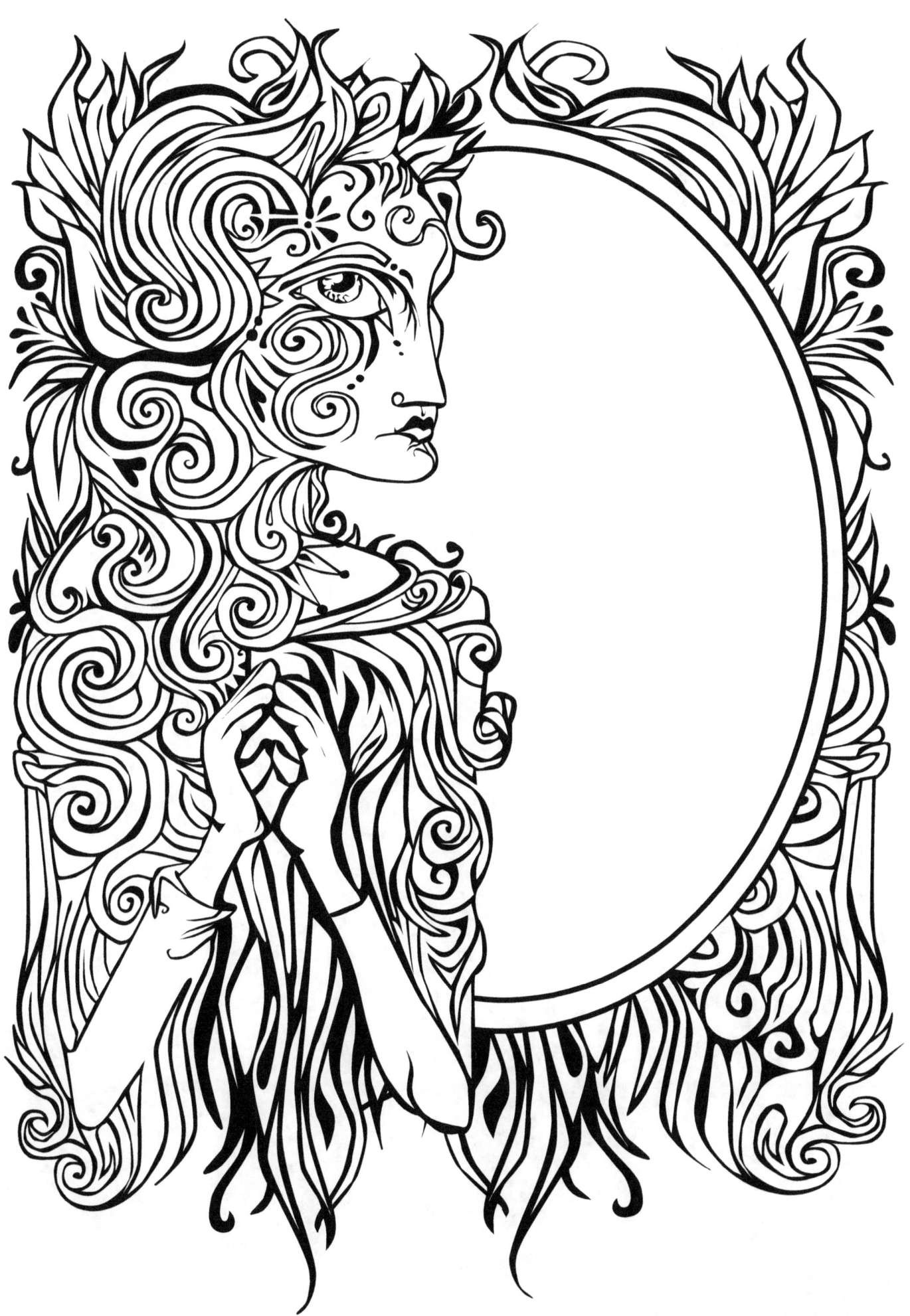

sigh...

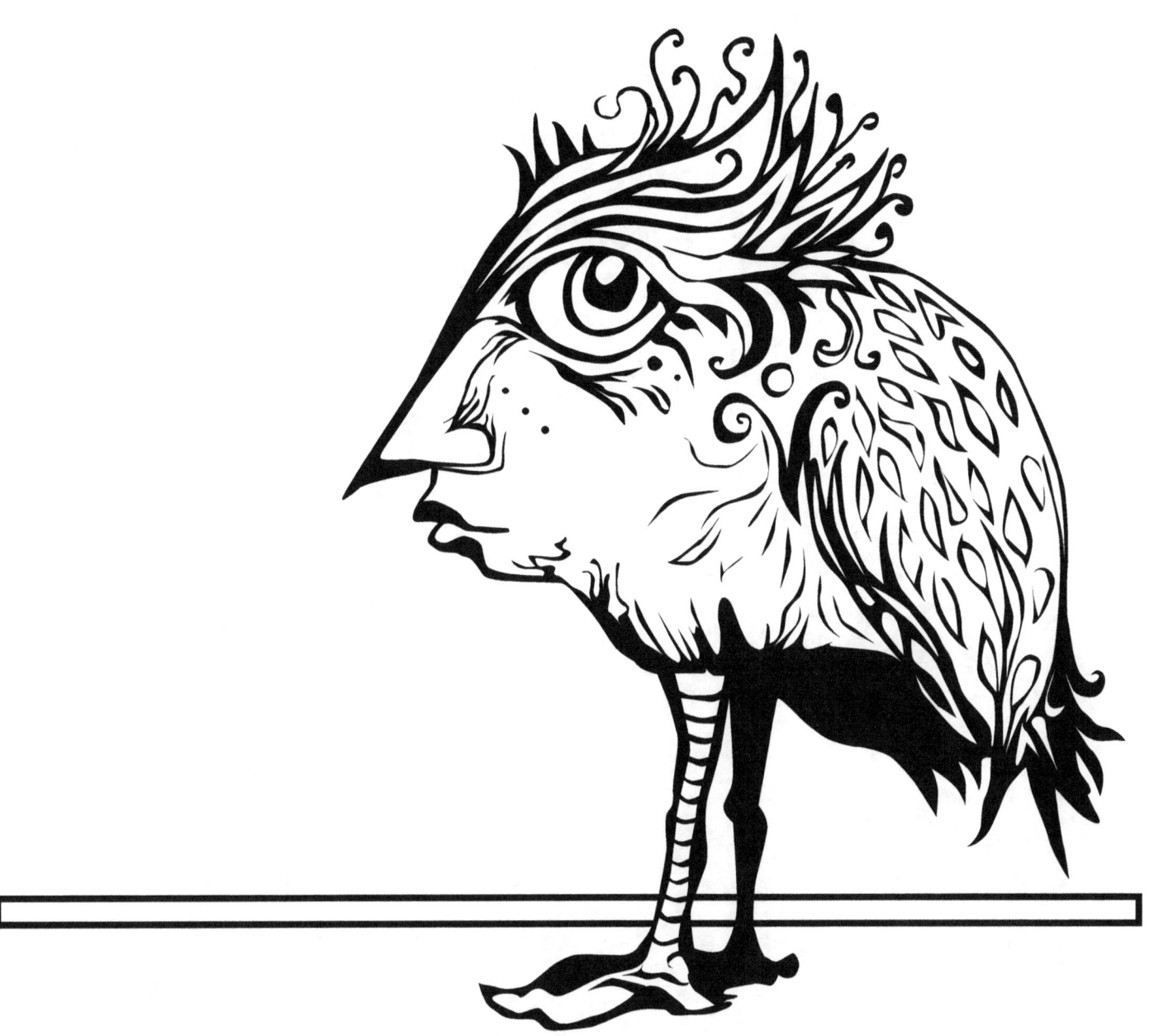

40

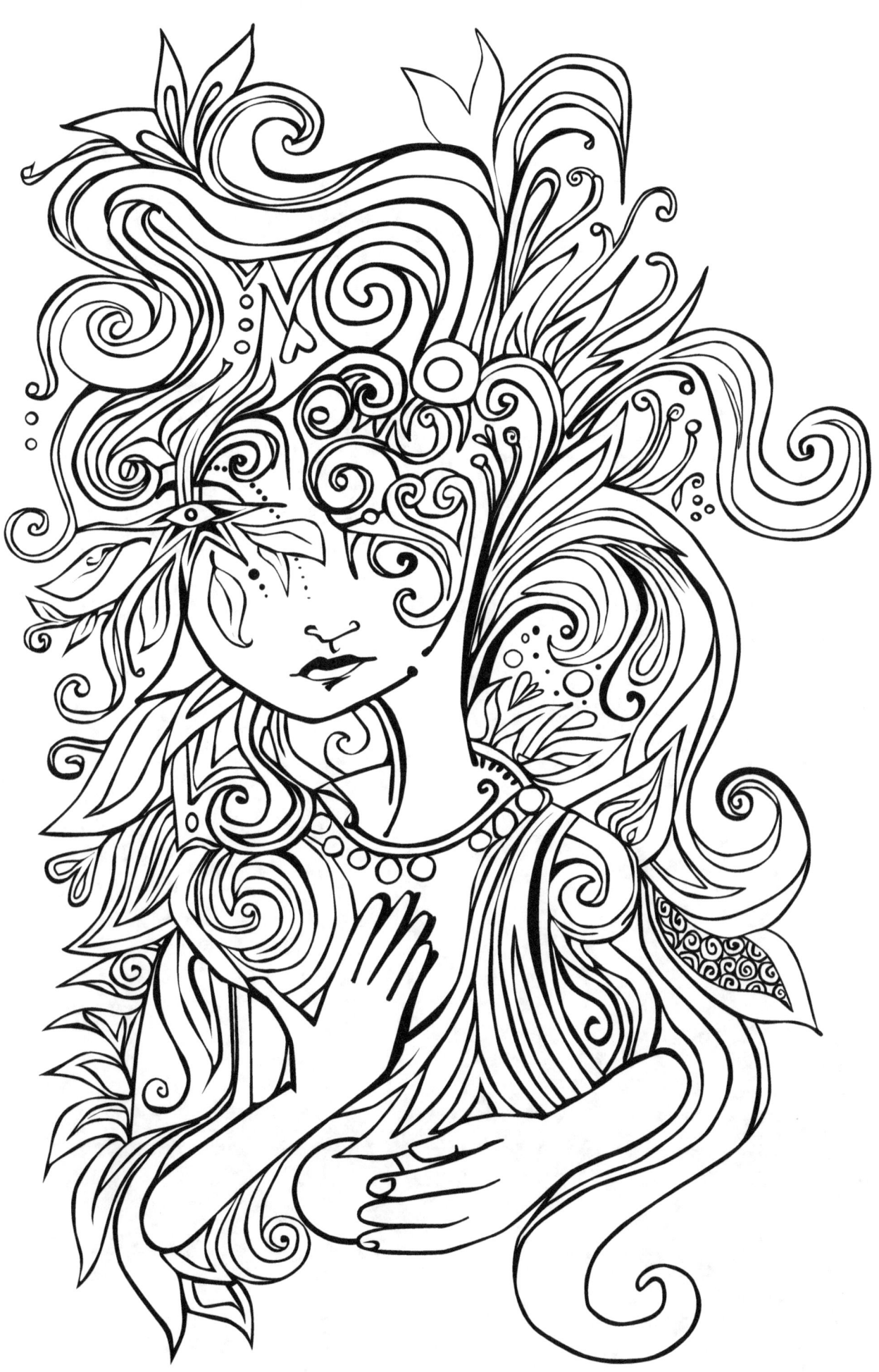

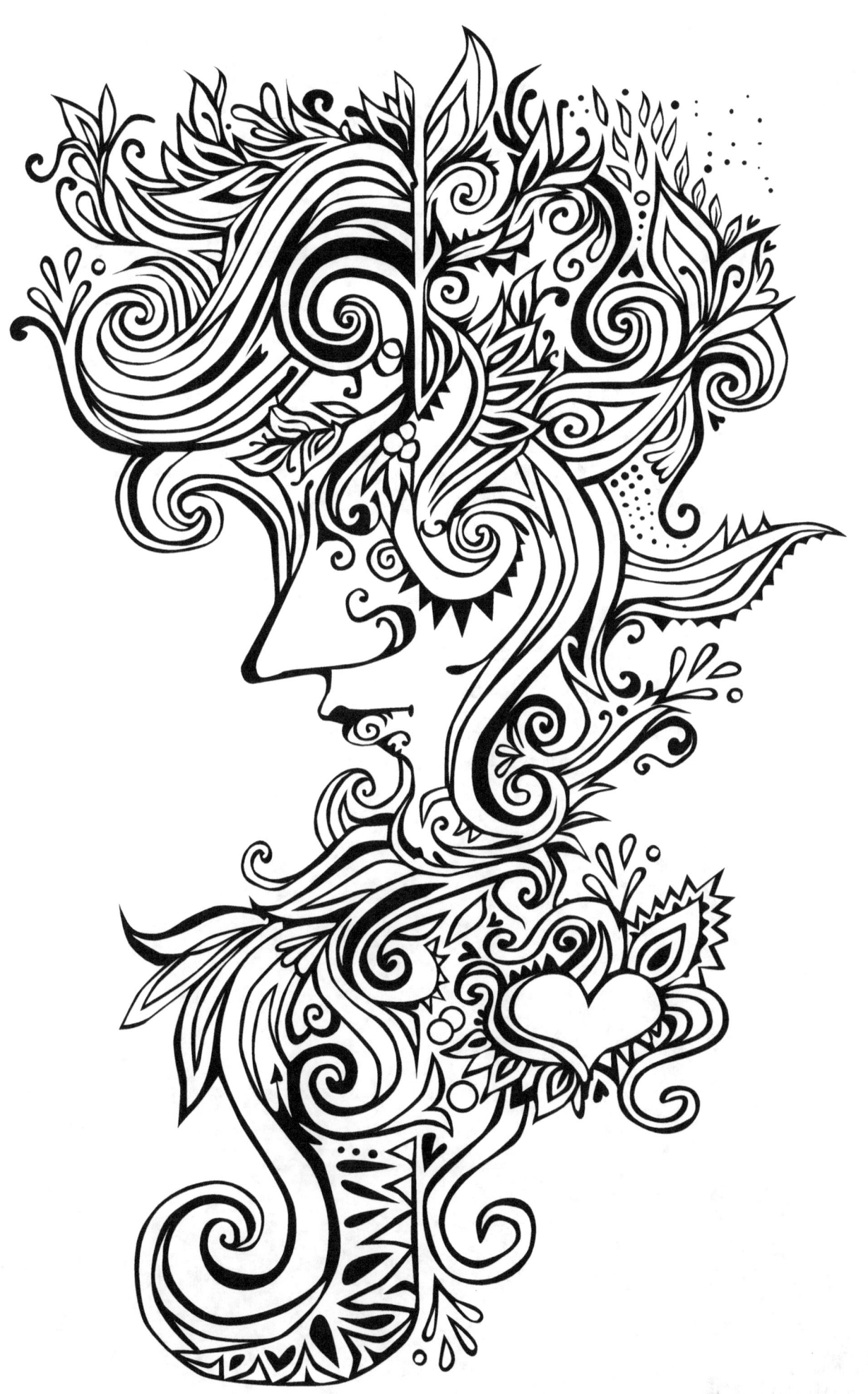